Nephi's Bow

written by Tiffany Thomas
illustrated by Nikki Casassa

CFI • An imprint of Cedar Fort, Inc. • Springville, Utah

HARD WORDS:
hunt, bow, break

PARENT TIP: Repeating the same books over and over again helps increase fluency and speed.

1

This is Nephi.

Nephi is
Lehi's son.

Nephi is a
man of God.

God tells
Nephi to go
with Lehi.

Nephi goes with Lehi.

God tells
Nephi to
hunt for food.

Nephi breaks his bow.

Lehi and his sons get mad.

Nephi makes
a new bow.

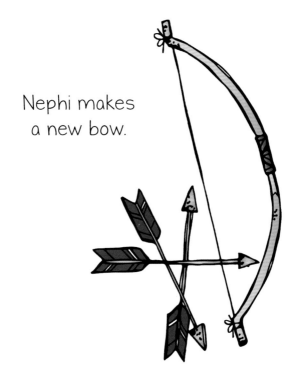

Nephi hunts
for food.

Lehi is not mad.

The end.

ISBN 13: 978-1-4621-4337-5

Published by CFI, an imprint of Cedar Fort, Inc. • 2373 W. 700 S., Suite 100, Springville, UT 84663
Distributed by Cedar Fort, Inc., www.cedarfort.com

Cover design and interior layout design by Shawnda T. Craig
Cover design © 2022 Cedar Fort, Inc.
Printed in China • Printed on acid-free paper
10 9 8 7 6 5 4 3 2 1